Original title:
The Orbit of Oddity

Copyright © 2025 Creative Arts Management OÜ
All rights reserved.

Author: Penelope Hawthorne
ISBN HARDBACK: 978-1-80567-877-9
ISBN PAPERBACK: 978-1-80567-998-1

The Uncharted Dance of Stars

In the sky where comets prance,
Asteroids in a silly trance.
Planets juggle, giggling loud,
While moons throw confetti in a crowd.

Saturn's rings spin like a top,
Neptune's whirl, a cosmic bop.
Each twirl sends a chuckling sound,
As starlit friends dance round and round.

Quasar Serenades Under Strange Skies

Quasars croon in gleeful tones,
With harmonies that tickle bones.
Shooting stars play tambourines,
While black holes share their silly scenes.

In galaxies where giggles bloom,
Oddities fill the cosmic room.
With every note, the cosmos beams,
As laughter flows like wild moonbeams.

Exploring the Fringe of Reality

Where logic bends and wobbles free,
Nonsense dances with glee.
Time skips rope, a playful game,
While gravity plays tricks, oh what a shame!

In realms where cats wear fancy hats,
And toast sings while the jazz beat pats.
Curiosity leads the way,
In this funny world where quirks hold sway.

Whirl of Whimsical Worlds

In a bubble where dreams collide,
Silly thoughts take a wild ride.
Jupiter bakes pies in the sun,
While Martian kids play hide and run.

Each planet spins with a quirky grin,
As comets race and twirl and spin.
The universe laughs, oh what a sight,
In this circus of cosmic delight!

Strange Harmonies of Heavens

In a galaxy where ducks can sing,
Stars dance and prance, a stellar fling.
Planets wear hats, all mismatched styles,
Cosmic giggles echo for miles.

Rockets jam out to a funky beat,
While comets tap dance on the celestial street.
Aliens play chess with their tentacled friends,
Laughing at rules that the universe bends.

Eclipses of the Mind

When thoughts collide like meteors bright,
Lunar laughter fills up the night.
Silly ideas float like wayward balloons,
Chasing shadows of cartoonish moons.

Lost in daydreams, I trip over stars,
Finding wisdom in bizarre guitar bars.
A brain full of jelly, oh what a sight,
When nonsense takes flight in the golden light.

Nebulous Revelations

In the clouds of wonder, secrets are spun,
Fizzing with magic, oh what fun!
Galactic giggles slip through the air,
As comical truths sparkle everywhere.

Whimsical whispers from behind a quasar,
"Why did the planet bring a guitar?"
Because in the vastness, laughter is key,
Even black holes yearn for comedy!

Gravity's Unravelled Secrets

Oh gravity, you tricky old friend,
You pull us down, then start to pretend.
With pies in the sky and squirrels on the moon,
We bounce around like a cartoon.

Lifting our spirits, we float in delight,
While aliens giggle at our silly flight.
Wobbling through quirks, we dance with glee,
In this wacky realm of zero G.

Journey of the Strange Starlings

In a world where starlings dance,
Around the moon, they twirl and prance.
With hats of cheese and shoes of jelly,
They bounce and jiggle, oh so smelly.

A comet sneezes, what a sight,
As giggles echo through the night.
With every quirk and wiggly flight,
They spin through laughter, pure delight.

Curious Pathways in Starlit Realms

Under skies that twist and bend,
Odd characters gather, no need to pretend.
With shoes tied together and hats askew,
They chase shooting stars and sip on dew.

A fish on a bicycle, clouds with grins,
In this odd realm, anything wins.
Step carefully on the paths of glee,
For every twist uncovers a mystery.

On the Edge of Infinite Peculiarity

Where gravity wobbles and planets sway,
Jellybeans rain on a sunny day.
With frogs on stilts and parrots that sing,
Life's a circus, let giggles take wing.

Bubblegum trees and candy cane streams,
In this topsy-turvy land of dreams.
There's no telling what you might find,
Curiosities await, uniquely designed.

Celestial Curiosities Collide

When planets collide with a cheerful thud,
And comets splat like a giant mud.
With bouncy bears and giggling moons,
They orchestrate odd and delightful tunes.

Each collision brings a chuckle or two,
As stardust twirls in a whimsical brew.
A dizzying dance of fun and surprise,
As the universe winks with mischievous eyes.

Dissonant Echoes in the Vast Sprawl

In a galaxy quite absurd,
A chicken danced with a bird.
They tried to sing a silly tune,
While juggling pies under the moon.

A cat in boots on a bright red bike,
Rode past a cow that played the pike.
The stars all laughed, a cosmic cheer,
As a toaster toasted without any fear.

Jellybeans bounced on a cosmic wave,
While fish wore hats, trying to behave.
They formed a band, quite out of place,
With a rubber duck leading the race.

Through the void, they twirled and spun,
Chasing comets, oh what fun!
In a peculiar world where things collide,
Laughter echoed, their joy the pride.

Frolics Beyond the Stars

In a realm where socks have legs,
And teacups dance like tiny pegs.
The sun wore shades, looking quite slick,
While robots told jokes and did a trick.

A space kangaroo hopped with glee,
Next to a tree that spoke like a bee.
They played hopscotch on rings of dust,
With a pickle that claimed to be a must.

Planets spun in a chaotic whirl,
As a rubber chicken began to twirl.
The comets cheered with a twinkling sound,
In this odd place, joy truly found.

So join the frolic, the cosmic fun,
Grab your oddities, everyone!
In this universe of silly delight,
Laughter shall shine, forever bright.

Wistful Whirlwinds of Time

Time flew past in a zany flight,
Chasing shadows, laughing bright.
Tick-tocks danced, a wobbly beat,
While silly squirrels skated on their feet.

A clock that winked with joking flair,
Spinning tales without a care.
Each second giggled, took a spin,
As goofball moments sought to win.

Days wore hats that looked quite strange,
Updated whims with every change.
In a whirlwind of fun and cheer,
Life's a merry prankster, dear!

So here we are in time's rush hour,
Frolicking with a quirky power.
With whimsy swirling all around,
In laughter's grip, we close the sound.

Stars That Spoke in Riddles

Once the stars began to chat,
With a giggle and a tip of a hat.
"What's your name?" the moonlight crooned,
As comets danced and planets swooned.

Constellations chuckled, oh so bright,
Can you guess our secret flight?
They whispered jokes on cosmic winds,
As cosmic clowns spun silly spins.

A riddle here, a pun or two,
The universe must love its crew.
Galaxies rolled with laughter's ray,
In the twinkling sky, they'd love to play.

So if you glance up at the night,
Join the stars in their merry flight.
Reveal the jokes they hide from sight,
And share their laughter, pure delight.

Forgotten Realms of the Night

In the shadows where giggles lurk,
Silly whispers start to work.
Moonbeams prance with playful glee,
In realms where oddities roam so free.

Forgotten corners hold their laughs,
With jumbled paths and wobbly halves.
Creatures chuckle, mischief steeped,
As night unravels what it keeps.

A castle made of candy dreams,
Where logic melts like ice cream streams.
Each room adorned with jest and jest,
In forgotten lands, the oddest fest.

So dance beneath the starlit haze,
In this realm of twisted ways.
For laughter waits on paths unseen,
In the night where misfits glean.

Starlight Stories of the Eccentric

Whimsical tales in starlight spread,
Of quirky heroes and bumpy threads.
A penguin wearing a top hat grand,
Sets out to juggle with one hand.

Once a cat decided to sing,
In the trees, it made hearts swing.
With mismatched socks and a bowtie too,
Its melodies brought joy anew.

In the circus of the cosmic breeze,
Strange delights are sure to tease.
Spaghetti hats and mismatched shoes,
In this universe, you cannot lose.

So raise a glass to tales untold,
Where every heartbeat breaks the mold.
In the folly of the universe wide,
Eccentric stories are our pride.

Serendipity Among the Stars

A penguin flew on a kite,
While jellybeans rained all night.
The moon wore glasses, quite askew,
Playing cards with a dancing crew.

A cat on Mars played the drums,
While laughing aliens danced like bums.
Comets raced with polka dots,
Spinning tales of cosmic plots.

Mysteries of the Unusual Skies

There's a squirrel with a telescope,
Searching for the stars of hope.
Balloons float on cereal seas,
Tickling the toes of bumblebees.

Planets wear the silliest hats,
While sunflowers giggle with the cats.
Juicy meteors fall like pie,
As clouds do cartwheels through the sky.

Eclipsing the Ordinary

A llama juggles shooting stars,
While noodles race in shiny cars.
Telephones chat with old-time clocks,
Dancing in their paper socks.

Cupcakes swim in milky way,
As hippos join the ballet play.
Worms in ties sell cosmic dreams,
In a world that bursts with seams.

Dreams Among Cosmic Eccentrics

A rabbit sings with cosmic flair,
While planets twirl without a care.
Stars wear shoes that squeak and pop,
As marshmallow clouds perform a hop.

Fish on stilts swim through the air,
Spreading joy with every flare.
Cheese moons glow in rainbow hues,
Inviting everyone to cruise.

Fables from Beyond the Cosmos

In a realm where cats drove cars,
And stars danced like they were at bars.
Planets wearing hats and shoes,
Juggled comets, sharing their news.

The aliens throw a wild bash,
With pluto-pies and meteor mash.
Space squids play the accordion loud,
While black holes twirl and spin around.

Each creature tells a tale unique,
Of chocolate moons and talking cheek.
The universe chuckles and glows,
As it listens close to these shows.

With laughter echoing through the void,
Imagination's vivid, overjoyed.
For cosmic fables twist and tease,
In the galaxy's quirky degrees.

Strange Loops of Light and Time

There once was a clock with no hands,
It tickled with joy, making new plans.
Hours flipped like pancakes in flight,
Flipping minutes from day into night.

Little bugs danced to the time's strange tune,
While frogs croaked rhymes with the light of the moon.
Time skipped like a rock on the pond,
In loops of laughter, we all responded.

Calendars giggled, refusing to age,
Writing their stories on a cosmic page.
Days turned to noodles, swirling in air,
As seconds joined hands, with nary a care.

And so the universe spun its delightful yarn,
Where logic vanished, and reasons were torn.
In this whimsical dance of light and sound,
Time's strange loops twist joyfully around.

Nahb of Nocturnal Nonsense

In the night where shadows do play,
The moon wears a tutu and twirls all day.
Owls wear glasses, sipping their tea,
Contemplating the meaning of three plus three.

Bats throw parties, hanging upside-down,
They wear tiny crowns and dance in the town.
Fireflies flash like disco balls bright,
As raccoons toast with their sparkling light.

A ghost in the corner tells puns galore,
As pumpkins giggle, begging for more.
The stars wink down with mischievous glee,
Plotting their pranks on the earthbound spree.

In this kingdom of night's silly quest,
Nonsensical creatures never take rest.
For laughter abounds under skies full of stars,
In a realm where weirdness eternally spars.

Kooky Cosmic Queries

Upon a comet, questions do float,
Like why do fish wear a tiny coat?
What do clouds drink when they're dry?
And why is the sky never shy?

Saturn wonders why its rings can't dance,
And if aliens ever wear pants.
Does the sun get dizzy in its flight?
Or does it giggle each day and night?

Astroids ponder the taste of cheese,
While nebulae swirl like a gentle breeze.
"Would you rather be a star or a stone?"
Questions bounce back in a cosmic tone.

So let's embrace these kooky delights,
In a universe swirling with curious sights.
For in the heart of the cosmic scene,
The joy of inquiry reigns, bright and serene.

Celestial Insanity

In a galaxy not so far,
Lived a moon with dreams bizarre.
It danced with stars, quite out of tune,
Singing silly songs to the sun and moon.

Planets wore mismatched socks,
Comets played hopscotch on time's blocks.
Uranus giggled, a cheeky sight,
While Saturn's rings spun left and right.

A spaceship tried to bake a pie,
But floated off, oh my, oh my!
The aliens tried to catch a star,
But ended up stuck in a jar.

In this chaos, joy will thrive,
As the universe laughs, feeling alive.
With quirks that dance through every night,
Celestial madness is pure delight.

Astrological Absurdities

Every horoscope has a twist,
Where Mercury's retro but can't resist.
Aries juggles celestial cheese,
While Libra floats on a cosmic breeze.

The stars have parties, oh what a sight,
With nebulae glimmering, colorful light.
Pisces swims in a bowl of soup,
As Virgo leads an odd dancing troupe.

In the zodiac, nonsense prevails,
With Martian ships full of cat-like whales.
Taurus snorts and rolls in delight,
Enjoying the madness that fills the night.

The cosmos spins with pillows of fluff,
As strange creatures laugh, saying, 'That's enough!'
In this realm of whimsical cheer,
Astrological absurdities bring us near.

Eccentrics of the Night Sky

Beneath the stars, oddballs converge,
With constellations singing their surge.
Sirius plays hide-and-seek with the sun,
While dwarf planet antics are just for fun.

A comet wears a polka dot hat,
While Mars debates with a wise old cat.
Galaxies twirl, creating a mess,
In their whimsical dance, more, more, no less.

Orion's belt has lost its buckle,
And the moon pulls pranks; oh what a chuckle!
A space pickle rolls down the Milky Way,
Chasing its dreams, in a silly ballet.

In this night sky, all is a game,
With laughter echoing in cosmic fame.
Eccentrics unite, both near and afar,
Celebrating nonsense like a shining star.

Tales from the Cosmic Fringe

From edges of space, stories unfold,
Of quirky beings, both brave and bold.
A rocket ship painted bright pink,
With aliens who dance and never sink.

UFOs going out for a stroll,
While planets in pajamas lose control.
Zany stars swapping secret jokes,
While Jupiter plays hide-and-seek with folks.

In the void, there's laughter to find,
With tales so twisted, you'll lose your mind.
Cosmic creatures share candy with glee,
As they float through the night on a jellyfish sea.

So gather 'round for a celestial yarn,
Of things that do giggle and sometimes brawn.
On the fringes, where weirdness reigns,
Tales unfold with winks and sprightly gains.

Astral Wonders and Marvels of the Wild

In a galaxy of quirks so bright,
Dancing stars play peek-a-boo at night.
Planets wear hats made of cheese,
While comets do the cha-cha with ease.

Aliens sip tea with grinning cats,
Juggling moons and ogling bats.
Nebulas twist like cotton candy,
And laughter echoes, sweet and dandy.

Excursions into Eccentric Skies

Shooting stars trip over their tails,
While rockets fly with silly sails.
A rainbow sloth on a swing up high,
Swings through puffs of marshmallow sky.

The sun wears glasses, looking quite cool,
Teaching planets how to be a fool.
The Milky Way spills cosmic milk,
A galaxy of giggles, smooth as silk.

The Miswritten Map of the Cosmos

Maps of stars that dance and sway,
Drawn by doodlers who lost their way.
Each X marks a spot where penguins glide,
While unicorns sail on a moonlit tide.

A journey through squiggles and loops,
Chasing the laughter of cosmic troops.
Navigating laughter with a wink,
In this odd space where thoughts are pink.

Unseen Wonders of the Night

In the quiet dark, oddities play,
Fireflies whisper to the night's ballet.
Cats in space wearing sky-blue shoes,
Play hopscotch on stardust and blues.

A shadow laughs, while crickets hum,
Jellyfish glow, a cosmic drum.
Wonders unseen, yet clearly felt,
In this swirl of joy, the night is spelt.

Gravity's Playful Anomalies

In a world where planets dance,
And moons wear goofy pants,
Saturn's rings spin out of line,
While comets sing and grace defines.

Jupiter wears a silly hat,
While asteroids on pogo sticks sat,
Stars giggle with a twinkling gleam,
In this cosmic, zany dream.

Oddities in Celestial Motion

A star once slipped on cosmic ice,
And tumbled past the pale moon's slice,
Mars threw a party, blowing up,
With aliens crashing in a cup.

Neptune's got a rubber duck,
Sailing in a whirl of luck,
Planets spin with moonlit glee,
Twisting sweetly through the spree.

Asteroids of Anomaly

Asteroids wear crooked ties,
As they zoom past velvet skies,
Laughing as they tumble through,
A cosmic rodeo, who knew?

With each wobbly, laugh-filled arc,
Space's a circus, bright and stark,
Galaxies break into a dance,
Leaving us in a hapless trance.

The Quirkiness of Celestial Wanderers

Venus lost her matching shoe,
Now wanders in a sky of blue,
Mercury's a speedy chap,
Wearing sunny socks with a flap.

Uranus spins with moonlit cheer,
Playing hide and seek with meteors near,
Stars clap hands in twinkling fun,
As comets whirl and races run.

Oddities in Motion

A penguin on a skateboard, zooming down the street,
Chasing after ice cream, oh what a silly feat!
Marshmallow moons are bouncing, all around the park,
While fireflies do the cha-cha, lighting up the dark.

A cat wearing a top hat, struts with such a flair,
With a monocle so cheeky and a cane without a care!
They dance on rainbow sidewalks, in a waltz so neat,
Where jellybeans rain down and everyone's on beat.

Galaxies of the Unusual

In a galaxy of wobble, where laughter's all abound,
Bouncing stars don't twinkle, they giggle all around!
A comet with a honk horn, zooms past with a cheer,
Spreading waves of happiness, to all who choose to steer.

In this land of quirk and puzzlement, cows do tango too,
In boots made out of donuts, 'neath skies of cotton blue!
They sing of cosmic wonders, in a language full of glee,
Where odd becomes the norm, and weird just lets you be.

Melodies of the Mysterious

A trumpet played by frogs, serenades the night,
With crickets on the tambourine, making quite a sight!
The moon swings in the rhythm, through clouds with every sway,
While stars join in the chorus, crafting dreams in play.

Balloons float in a symphony, taking off in pairs,
With rubber ducks conducting, beneath the giggling flares!
The notes, like candy laughter, fill the air so sweet,
In this whimsical universe, where all the oddities meet.

Odd Celestial Journeys

A snail with a jetpack zooms across the space,
Chasing after meteors, in a silly race!
Invisible space squirrels toss acorns like confetti,
In this curious cosmos, where the odd is always ready.

With a spaceship made of pizza, we sail the starry sea,
Searching for the giggle-bots, come join us, won't you plea?
Through wormholes filled with laughter, we travel near and far,
In our funny little cosmic ride, aboard the jolly car!

Cosmic Oddfellows in Flight

In a rocket made of bubblegum,
Two squirrels dream of hitting the sun.
They spin and twirl in zero-g,
While sipping tea and counting bees.

A cat in a space suit sings a tune,
With a dandelion hat, he'll dance 'til noon.
His whiskers twitch as he starts to glide,
Past a comet that's taking a slide.

Jellybeans rain from the starry sky,
As frogs in top hats hop up high.
What a sight, what a mess, what a cosmic show,
In this wacky world, they steal the glow.

Each loop and spin, a laughter spree,
In a universe where all are free.
So toast with your juice and take to the night,
With cosmic oddfellows in joyous flight.

Twilight Travelers Through the Unusual

At twilight, the balloons begin to tease,
With giggles rising on the cosmic breeze.
A penguin plays chess with a clever fox,
While stars wink softly in their socks.

Through mirrors of dreams, where time runs amok,
A llama in sneakers takes a wild walk.
Each step a stumble, each laugh a cheer,
In a realm where absurdity's near.

A dinosaur with a cape, feeling grand,
Takes a selfie with clouds, so close at hand.
Tickling planets as they float by,
In this twilight dance, oh my, oh my!

Through the vastness, the humor takes flight,
In this world where oddness shines bright.
With twinkling stars and colors so bold,
The night is a story waiting to be told.

Cosmic Whispers in the Abyss

In the abyss where whispers are loud,
A jellyfish leads a curious crowd.
With tentacles dancing, they sway to the beat,
Of a comet that juggles, oh what a treat!

A walrus with glasses deciphers the stars,
While a hedgehog in sandals claims cosmic cars.
They race through the void, in galactic delight,
Silly critters making the dark feel bright.

Bubbles of laughter float all around,
As aliens groove to an earthling sound.
With moonbeams as props and asteroids as chairs,
They throw a party, laughter fills the airs.

Through the cosmic sea, where shadows so sway,
Oddities find a place for play.
In whispers so funny, in shades of the night,
The abyss sparkles with pure delight.

Celestial Eccentricities

In a space disco, the planets revolve,
With dancers in tutus, a problem to solve.
The sun runs a marathon, shiny and bright,
While the moons try to keep up, what a funny sight!

A rabbit jumps ropes with Saturn's rings,
As Earth plays the drums and happily sings.
Shooting stars twirl in a pirouette,
Cosmic ballet, best show on the set!

Giggles erupt as the meteors race,
While aliens pop corn, oh what a place!
With snacks from the comets, it's all quite absurd,
In this realm where the laughter's unheard.

Each quirk and twist of the celestial dance,
Entries of humor that invite a chance.
In this theater of light, where oddities thrive,
The universe chuckles, asking us to jive.

Starlit Idylls and Oddities

In a galaxy of misfits, they play,
Juggling comets that chase the day.
Stars giggle about their crooked lines,
While the moons dance with mismatched twines.

Space squirrels plot their nutty quests,
Wearing helmets made of old tin vests.
They surf on rays from suns gone wild,
While aliens laugh with a playful smile.

Gravity's laughing, taking a break,
As black holes prank with a cosmic shake.
Planets wear hats, spinning in glee,
In a kookie world, forever carefree.

Each star whispers secrets, out of sync,
While gravity pulls at all we think.
In this realm where oddities reign,
The universe chuckles, again and again.

Wandering Planets of Peculiar Dreams

A planet rolls with an uneven trot,
Dancing in circles, oh what a plot!
Saturn's rings are a carousel ride,
While Jupiter giggles, quite full of pride.

In nebulas bright, fashion takes flight,
Where stardust dresses get a new sight.
Laughter erupts from the cosmic crowd,
As meteors sing, both silly and loud.

Uranus shows off with a jester's flair,
While Venus plays tag with an asteroid fair.
Silly comets toss confetti in wake,
For the dreamers who drift through cosmic lakes.

The sun winks down with a mischievous glow,
While planets parade in a bonkers show.
In this funny realm of galactic schemes,
They're chasing their whims in peculiar dreams.

Serendipity Among the Spheres

In a realm where oddballs take flight,
Planets spin tales both day and night.
A moonbeam giggles as it skips by,
While stars throw shade in a twinkling tie.

Jupiter's swirls wear polka dot socks,
While Saturn's rings hold tea with the cocks.
Cosmic kites fly with whimsical grace,
Chasing the laughter through infinite space.

A starfish floats in a pool of stars,
Dreaming of riding wild meteors' cars.
Galactic hamsters run marathons of cheer,
With space donuts flying, oh what a year!

Laughter erupts from a comet's bright tail,
As oddities dance in a cosmic ale.
In this joyful dance among the spheres,
The galaxy giggles, washing away fears.

Uncharted Skies

Beyond the stars, in uncharted air,
Wanderers find their rhythm and flair.
Frisky asteroids play hide and seek,
While stardust kids giggle and squeak.

Floating on bubbles of dreamy delight,
Moons tell stories that stretch the night.
With candy-flavored clouds that drift slow,
Winning wishes that twinkle and glow.

Galactic giraffes reach for the sun,
While space pirates laugh, having so much fun.
In a goofy waltz of celestial cheer,
They share their secrets, loud and clear.

With a wink from the cosmos, all seems right,
As every twinkle brings joy to the night.
In this playground where quirks intertwine,
The uncharted skies forever shine.

Celestial Whimsy

Stars play hopscotch in the night,
Comets wear hats, oh what a sight.
Planets spin on candy floss,
In this universe, we've all come across.

Asteroids giggle as they fly,
Winking at each other, oh my!
Moonbeams tickle with gentle grace,
In this silly, starry space.

Science books can't define this fun,
Where gravity choses to run.
Galaxies swirl in a jiggle dance,
As cosmic beings take their chance.

So let the night be filled with glee,
In a weird and wild jubilee.
For in the vast, enchanted space,
Laughter holds a special place.

Unraveling Cosmic Threads

Twirling yarns of stardust bright,
Knitting socks of sheer delight.
Wormholes play hide and seek,
While black holes giggle and peek.

Nebulas wear their fluffy coats,
As space-time sails in paper boats.
Aliens bake pies with strange zest,
In the universe's ever-quirky fest.

Gravity's a trickster, what a tease,
Pulling you close, then saying, "Please!"
With donuts orbiting in a loop,
Join the cosmic culinary troupe!

Stars hold hands in a jumping race,
While supernovae laugh in grace.
Each thread we unravel, oh what a scene,
In this weird cosmos, we're all part of the dream.

Dancing Through the Eccentric Void

Planets strut in sequined suits,
Asteroids join with squeaky boots.
Doing the tango on a solar flare,
What a sight; you'd stop and stare!

Quasars twirl with a dazzling grin,
While cosmic dust makes a spin.
Galaxies burst into a wild spin,
As space-time lets the party begin.

Fluffy comets toss confetti bright,
While starlings plan a space delight.
Helium balloons float near the sun,
Creating laughter, oh what fun!

With eclipses serving as the DJ's spin,
Let the dancing in the cosmos begin.
In this void bizarre, we find our joy,
Celebrating life, oh what a ploy!

Whispers of the Quirky Cosmos

Whispers travel on a light beam,
Telling tales of a cosmic dream.
Jupiter wears its swirling hat,
As Saturn chuckles, "What's up with that?"

Funky exchanges from star to star,
Chasing meteors racing afar.
Each twinkling light has a funny story,
In this celestial parody of glory.

Planets swap snacks in a grand buffet,
"Try my rings," they shout; "What a display!"
Neutron stars crack silly jokes,
While black holes share stories of folks.

So listen close to the cosmic treat,
In every whisper, a joyful beat.
For in the vastness, where quirkiness roams,
Laughter echoes, finding its homes.

Moonlight and Marvels

Bouncing beams in the night sky,
Chasing fireflies that whisper by.
Lunar rabbits tell tales of cheese,
While stars giggle in cosmic tease.

Juggling planets in a dance so bright,
Waltzing comets in sheer delight.
Meteor showers rain down with flair,
Laughter echoes from the solar air.

Rockets dressed in polka dots zoom,
While moonbeams gather in a room.
Galactic games make shadows bend,
As twilight bids the day to end.

So here's to dreams that twirl and spin,
In a universe where chaos wins.
Join the fun, let your spirits soar,
In this cosmic carnival, forevermore.

Wobbling Worlds

Planets play a topsy-turvy game,
One named Bob, and one named Flame.
They trip and tumble, laugh and roll,
Bouncing light like a jolly shoal.

Galaxies giggle, twirling around,
As asteroids hop with a happy sound.
Stars dressed in hats, strut on by,
While UFOs wave, oh me, oh my!

Nebulas swirl in a cotton candy clip,
Space walruses take a sliding trip.
With cosmic pies they fiercely toss,
In this wild realm, there's no such loss.

So grab your boots, take off your frown,
In wobbly worlds, there's no time to drown.
Laughter ripples through the keen expanse,
Join the waltz of the space-time dance.

Celestial Curiosities

A curious star with a quirky grin,
Petting a comet while spinning in.
Astro-kittens chasing solar rays,
Playing hide and seek for days and days.

Venus in a wig, giving cosmic winks,
Mars, the artist, paints purple drinks.
Jupiter's belly shakes from thrills,
As Saturn debates the best ice creams and frills.

Space cows mooing in milky ways,
Lunar llamas enjoying sun rays.
Each curious quirk brings laughter anew,
Where stardust antics can shine right through.

So zip along on this cosmic spree,
Where oddities bloom, and hearts run free.
In starlit corners, joy finds a way,
In celestial weirdness, we're here to stay.

The Enigma Beyond

In shadows cast by a wobbly sun,
Mysteries swirl, and fun's begun.
Gravity giggles as it jumps,
While laughter echoes in all the thumps.

Time flies backward, a silly affair,
Chasing its tail without a care.
Dancing safely on a comet's back,
While mysteries tumble in a starry pack.

Space junkies trade their wildest dreams,
For muddy thoughts and bubblegum schemes.
Whispers of wonders float through the air,
Tickling toes, if you dare to share.

So come explore this enigma's bright,
With peculiar things that bring delight.
Where laughter twinkles in the galactic sea,
Join in the fun—come frolic with me!

Eclectic Echoes of Infinity

In a world where umbrellas fly,
Cats wear hats and dogs ask why.
Backwards clocks tick to the beat,
As penguins skate on icy street.

Toasters toast with a cheeky grin,
While goldfish dance and violins spin.
Marshmallows bounce on jelly beans,
Underneath the moon's funny gleams.

Llamas debate the meaning of cake,
While chairs plot schemes they'll never make.
A flying toaster squeaks with glee,
In this odd land of jubilee.

So twist your thoughts, let laughter unfold,
In this realm where life is bold.
Embrace the quirks, enjoy the jest,
For in the strange, we are the best!

Quaint Views from the Cosmos

Balloons drift past the starry lane,
As squirrels knit in spaceships' train.
Wormholes giggle, planets play,
With candy comets on display.

Aliens wear socks with stripes,
Disco balls and light-up pipes.
A fish swims by in a tuxedo,
Chasing stars like a bold torpedo.

Jupiter juggles, Saturn spins,
While Martians laugh at their own sins.
Galaxies bloom in polka dots,
In this universe of silly plots.

So take a peek, and don't you frown,
The cosmos wears a funny crown.
With whimsy bright in every nook,
Adventure waits in every book.

Dance of the Cosmic Oddballs

Dancing noodles float in cheer,
While cupcakes toast with juice and beer.
A rubber chicken leads the way,
With funky moves that brighten day.

Planets twirl in silly glee,
Stars waltz with silly degree.
A jellybean band plays out of tune,
While Marvin the Martian croons to the moon.

Asteroids tap like feisty cats,
With alien friends and moonlit hats.
Gravity giggles as it sways,
In a kaleidoscope of cosmic plays.

So join the fun, shake off the dust,
In this odd dance, it's a must.
With laughter echoing through the night,
Let joy take wing and take flight!

Bizarre Dimensions in the Void

In a space where cheese is king,
And cookie monsters flap and sing.
Upside-down flowers twist and yawn,
On a path where colors spawn.

A rabbit juggles planets bright,
While sunglasses gleam in the starlight.
Frogs recite Shakespeare in tune,
Bouncing high, beneath the moon.

Here, laughter echoes off the walls,
As time itself plays silly thralls.
Gummy bears dance with light bulbs bright,
Creating speculations of delight.

So roam these lanes, let whimsy thrive,
Among the odd where dreams arrive.
In this bizarre, plushy embrace,
Find joy lurking in every space.

Quasar Quirks

In a galaxy far with a twisty face,
Stars juggle planets in a zany race.
Comets wear hats, what a sight to see,
While aliens sip tea, so fancy and free.

Gravity's giggles, they bounce all around,
Meteors dance in a silly sound.
Quasars are quirky with lights that flick,
Making jokes with the moon, a cosmic trick.

Bizarre Constellations

Ursa Major is lost, playing hide and seek,
While Orion's belt tightens; it's feeling weak.
Pisces splashes water in a bubble bath,
And Taurus the bull is just taking a math.

A triangle's grinning, a circle's gone mad,
With square stars arguing, isn't that bad?
In this wild night, the sky wears a grin,
As stars spill secrets, let the fun begin!

Lunar Lullabies in Dissonance

The moon hums tunes in a wobbly key,
With starlit choirs singing off a tree.
Craters are giggling; they can't hold still,
As shadows dance out on a lunar hill.

Night skies are laughing, they can't hide the glee,
While meteors fashion a grand jubilee.
Rockets that hiccup, balloon-like they rise,
Crashing the rhythm, to everyone's surprise!

Cosmic Fables of the Uncommon

Once a star wandered, lost and confused,
Mistook a black hole for a friendly muse.
It spun tales of journeys, so twistedly vain,
While satellites snickered, hiding their pain.

Cows mooed in space, on rockets they flew,
In patches of stardust, sipping on dew.
So gather round folks, for stories of old,
Where laughter and quirks in the cosmos unfold.

Quirks in the Galaxy's Dance

In a corner of space, the comets conspire,
They twirl and they spin, never tire.
A planet in blue wears a silly hat,
While asteroids gather for a cosmic chat.

Stars snicker and giggle, they glow in delight,
As meteors tease in a theatrical flight.
Saturn's rings jingle, a musical spree,
Orions are laughing, as wild as can be.

The moons make a ruckus, a playful brigade,
In a waltz of the weird, no rules to invade.
Space donkeys trot with laughter so bright,
In the silly bazaar of the starry night.

Galactic jesters with wands made of light,
Prank the black holes, what a curious sight!
A nebula chuckles, so fluffy and bold,
In the whimsical universe, stories unfold.

Peculiar Paths of Stardust

A star wore SOCKS in its fiery domain,
While planets played tag in the cosmic rain.
Comets with candy, all sugary sweet,
In this realm, laughter travels on light's fleet.

Black holes are ponders with hats on their heads,
Whispering secrets where spacetime dreads.
Neutron stars bouncing, they hop and they leap,
Twinkling with laughter, their secrets they keep.

Asteroids waddle, they're walking with flair,
In a jig with the photons, beyond compare.
Galaxies giggle in swirling ballet,
In the quirky expanse where the odd always play.

A supernova sneezes, stars scatter like seeds,
While stardust confetti covers all cosmic needs.
Nighttime is silly, the universe plays,
In this tapestry woven through whimsical ways.

Astral Anomalies

In the cosmos where humor takes flight,
Quasars are baking a cosmic cake right.
With sprinkles of light from a jovial sun,
The galaxies gather for fun's chosen run.

Planets in huddles, each one with a quirk,
Dance silly steps with the Milky Way's smirk.
A comet's a jester, with jokes in its tail,
While starlight is giggling, it's utterly pale.

Meteor showers rain down a funny spree,
Where shooting stars wish for simple glee.
Pulsars keep time, but in beats that are strange,
As cosmic navigators not worried to change.

Asteroids boogie, their moves are divine,
Space-time is a riot, it twists like a vine.
Out here in the endless, the odd is the norm,
As we surf the starlight, we happily swarm.

Gravity's Unusual Embrace

Bouncing through the cosmos, a dance full of glee,
Planets in hugs, so oddly carefree.
Gravity teases, pulling stars to the ground,
In this wobbly space where laughter is found.

Dancing nebulae swirl, what a sight to behold,
With jokes in their colors, bright hues made of gold.
A cheerful black hole takes everyone in,
With a wink and a smile, let the fun begin.

Astrolabes giggle, charting paths with flair,
While satellites play hopscotch in nebulous air.
Cosmic confetti falls, a vibrant cascade,
In a universe crazy that has no charade.

With each funny twist, new oddities show,
Where planets collide in a rare cosmic glow.
Gravity's grip has a knack for delight,
In this jolly old dance, we're all stars tonight.

Whims of the Wandering Stars

Stars wearing hats, strutting about,
Playing hopscotch, oh, what a clout!
Dancing in circles, dizzy and bright,
They giggle and twirl, all through the night.

Comets with tails made of candy floss,
Swirling and twirling, a whimsical toss!
Planets in parties, galactic parade,
Like a cosmic circus, grandly displayed.

Nebulas winking in colors so bold,
Sharing their secrets, funny tales told.
Asteroids stumbling, a fumble and roll,
Each snapshot a laugh, oh, what's the toll?

With laughter galore, the void takes a spin,
In this jolly sky, we're all sure to win!
Shooting stars zooming, do you hear them sing?
In this madcap jest, joy takes to wing.

Chasing Shadows of Peculiarity

Shadows in sneakers, running quite free,
Chasing reflections behind the old tree.
With giggles and laughs, they dart in and out,
Creating a ruckus, there's no doubt!

Bouncing like gumdrops, the moon can't stay,
As shadows imitating dance have their play.
While whispers and chuckles float through the air,
Oddities twirl with an eccentric flair.

Strange creatures tumble, one-footed and hefty,
They juggle the stars, not quite deftly.
Laughter erupts as they trip on a grin,
In this world of odd, where do we begin?

Where shadows embrace the unusual scene,
Chasing their wild dreams, bright and serene.
In the glow of the night, life's a silly game,
And chasing these shadows, we're all just the same.

Convoluted Routes of Light

Squiggly lines dance in the night sky,
Light beams with energy, oh me, oh my!
Paths that twist like a curly fry,
Let's trace the route where giggles fly!

Zigzagging photons, they race with a grin,
Bouncing off planets, let the fun begin!
A maze of bright laughter, what a delight,
Where paths overlap, in giggles ignite.

Twisted and turned, each journey's a jest,
Riddles of lumens, they never do rest.
With sparkles and giggles, they flit to and fro,
A party in motion, putting on a show!

So leap through this path where the light looks bizarre,
Share joy with reflections from each noisy star.
In this tangled web, let's dance as we please,
Amidst routes of laughter that flow in the breeze.

Fractals of the Extraordinary

Shapes that repeat, like a cosmic surprise,
With each twist and turn, the humor soon flies.
Mirthful designs with a curious flair,
Painting the cosmos, it's a sight rare!

Splendidly silly, they wiggle and squirm,
Fractals that giggle, all wobbly and firm.
In intricate patterns, chuckles emerge,
As oddities play and silly things surge.

Fabulous visions in loops are displayed,
Tickling the senses, a joyful charade.
Each fractal a smile, with layers gone wild,
Wondering how much even space has smiled!

So let's dive into this whimsical dance,
Where the extraordinary gives us a chance.
To laugh with the patterns, lost in the light,
In fractals of joy, everything feels right.

Luminous Oddballs in the Milky Way

There's a star that wears a hat,
Spinning round with a cheeky chat.
Planets dance in silly lines,
Making faces, like little mines.

A comet struts with sparkly tails,
While meteors tell curious tales.
Nebulae giggle in colors bright,
Joking around through the deep night.

Asteroids play tag in space,
Gravitational games make a race.
With a wink and a funny shout,
They whirl and twirl, no doubt!

In this galaxy of goofy glee,
Silly antics we can see.
Cosmic humor fills the air,
Luminous oddballs everywhere!

Beyond the Norm of Celestial Bodies

Here's a planet with polka dots,
Wobbling 'round in all the spots.
Its friends join in, with stripes so bold,
A fashion show that never gets old.

Saturn wears mismatched rings,
While buzzing moons do silly flings.
Asteroids laugh as they collide,
In a cosmic funfair, side by side.

Galaxies twist like a wiggly dance,
Inviting all into their chance.
Gravity pulling, but with a grin,
They keep on laughing, it's a win!

Beyond the norm, they have their way,
In strange attire they sing and sway.
In a universe full of fun,
Every oddball shines like the sun!

Magnetism of the Uncommon

There's a star that attracts with a wink,
Pulling in comets quicker than you think.
With a beam so quirky, it shines through,
Laughing as it collects its crew.

Mysterious orbs dance in delight,
While space dust sparkles, oh what a sight!
A swirling mass of strange allure,
Uncommon ties that are ever pure.

A black hole burps, it's quite the sound,
Swallowing all that comes around.
In gravity's grip, they laugh and sway,
Magnetism leading the odd ballet.

In this realm where weirdos gleam,
Every quirk is embraced like a dream.
Celestial bodies break the mold,
Magnetism of the uncommon, so bold!

Whirlwind of the Idiosyncratic

Out in space, there's a quirky breeze,
Tickling stars and teasing trees.
Planets spin in a dizzy line,
Swooping low in a funny design.

A moon with a mustache grins wide,
While suns run races, full of pride.
Quasars chuckle, bright with delight,
In this whirlwind, all seems right.

Galactic giggles swirl around,
While asteroids hop like they've found ground.
Pulsars blink in a rhythmic cheer,
Drawing all the oddballs near.

In this space of the odd and strange,
Adventure awaits around every range.
The idiosyncratic finds its flow,
In a cosmic party, stealing the show!

Strange Allure of the Blue Horizon

There's a fish wearing socks on the beach,
A penguin in heels, with a grand orange peach.
The clouds are made of bubble gum, oh my,
And whales are dancing, waving goodbye.

Seagulls are singing in perfect tune,
While cats play chess under the bright moon.
Kangaroos shuffle, wearing bright hats,
At the disco, where time travels like bats.

Stars wink like jesters, they giggle and twirl,
While space-fairing monkeys do barrel rolls and swirl.
In this place, nothing's ever quite sane,
A silly adventure, where laughs reign supreme.

Oh, laughter erupts in the echoes of night,
As the sun yawns wide and prepares for flight.
In the bizarre, the cheer never ends,
Inviting all beings, to be my friends.

Luminance in the Quirkiverse

Light bulbs wear glasses and can't see the glow,
While fried eggs paint rainbows, putting on a show.
A snail's in a hurry with rollerblade shoes,
Speeding past kittens in glittering hues.

Toasters hold parties with dance and with cheers,
As pancakes flip high, defying their fears.
Unicorns prance through the syrupy mist,
Where jelly beans jive, they can't be missed.

In a realm where shadows create silly plots,
The lamps turn to dancers, doing the bots.
With giggles like rain and bubbles like dreams,
This nutty dimension bursts at the seams.

Join the frolic in this whimsical land,
Life's a mad caper, all carefully planned.
Spin around once, let your cares float away,
In the quirkiverse, we dance and play!

Dawn of the Disparate Celestials

At dawn, the moon wears a fluffy white coat,
And stars ride on comets, oh what a note!
The sun sips tea with the wandering breeze,
In a park where the grass grows at odd angles, with ease.

A fox in suspenders recites a fine rhyme,
As the ticklish toadstools giggle in time.
Jellyfish stroll with their arms in a sway,
Beneath the sky where squid frolic all day.

Skyscrapers tumble like playful larva,
In lands where nobody follows the karma.
Like socks lost in dryers, the colors are frayed,
Endless jesters laugh as the parade is displayed.

When dawn rises up with a chuckle and grin,
A strange jubilation wraps all that's within.
Each moment is madness, and yet it feels right,
In the dawn of the disparate, everything's bright.

Forgotten Dreams of Cosmic Oddity

In a garden of noodles, the aliens cheer,
With cupcakes for chairs, oh what a frontier!
A clock ticks backward, making no sense,
While stars wear pajamas and bathtubs dispense.

Clouds have mustaches, their laughter contagious,
A donut-shaped planet, so truly outrageous.
Marshmallow trees sway to a soft funky beat,
Where robots do tango, a dance that's quite sweet.

Frogs take to surfing, riding silver waves,
While old shoes collect tales from curious graves.
Kites made of pickle float up to the sky,
In a world made of quirks, where norms are awry.

Forgotten are dreams from the realms of routine,
In this playground of wits and the bold and pristine.
Step forth and let whimsy dictate your roam,
In the cosmic ballet, come find your home.

Celestial Ballad of the Unusual

Stars dance in polka dots,
Planets wear mismatched socks.
Asteroids sing silly tunes,
Comets throw goofy rocks.

Uranus spins with a grin,
While Venus pretends to frown.
Saturn's rings do the hula,
While Mars just turns around.

Galaxies giggle and spin,
Swirling in spirals of cheer.
Cosmic clowns in a parade,
Float through the sky far and near.

In this universe of jest,
Every quasar has a quirk.
Laughter echoes through the stars,
In the cosmic comic work.

Anomalies in the Twilight Sky

A star wore a silly hat,
While meteors danced a jig.
Constellations misbehave,
Playing tag at the summit big.

The moon made a face at night,
Winking at a passing star.
Jupiter juggled its moons,
As they twirled near and far.

Satellites snicker and twirl,
Spinning tales of delight.
Even comets can't resist,
A good laugh in their flight.

With a wink and a twirl,
Celestial wonders collide.
In the sky, humor's embrace,
Makes the stargazers abide.

Explorations in the Realm of the Strange

Black holes wear oversized shoes,
While quasars pull funny pranks.
Nebulae puff out big clouds,
Creating cosmic out-of-thanks.

Twirling moons in clownish garb,
Squirt each other with stardust.
Galactic jokes about dark matter,
In this realm, we always trust.

Time travelers trip on their feet,
Falling through wormholes with grace.
Punchlines echo in the void,
As they vanish without a trace.

With a flicker and a blink,
The universe flips on a dime.
Laughter reigns in strange places,
Making oddity seem sublime.

Nebulae of the Unfamiliar

Floofy clouds in vibrant hues,
Mysterious shapes and sounds.
Galaxy jesters spin their tales,
As they gather cosmic crowns.

A pulsar gave us a thumbs up,
While black holes played peekaboo.
Stardust swirled like cotton candy,
In this carnival for two.

Comets with colorful trails,
Racing across the cosmic lanes.
With giggles and gleeful winks,
They romp through stellar domains.

Luminous laughter fills the void,
As planets play hide and seek.
In this bizarre, funny wonder,
We find joy among the unique.

Irregular Rhythms of the Universe

In the sky, things dance around,
Planets spin without a sound.
A comet trips, then does a twist,
While aliens laugh, 'Did you see that?!'

Stars wear socks, and moons do prance,
Shooting stars join in the dance.
Gravity's gone off for a break,
As meteors perform and quake.

Celestial Puzzles and Paradoxes

What's that constellation doing there?
A triangle wearing mismatched hair.
Jupiter sings, while Saturn buzzes,
In this galactic game of puzzles.

Black holes playing hide and seek,
Wormholes popping out to speak.
In a world where things don't fit,
Oh, the cosmic comedy of it!

Oddities Above the Familiar

A starfish caught in a cosmic net,
Winks at Earth, a grand duet.
Clouds wear hats, totally off beat,
Sunny rays march in tiny feet.

The sun tells jokes from dawn to dusk,
While planets giggle, their voices husk.
Aliens play hopscotch in the night,
While we look up, filled with delight.

Anomalous Orbits and Tales

There is a tale of a rogue moon,
Who danced away to a silly tune.
Her friends shouted, 'Where's she gone now?'
While black holes laughed, 'Just take a bow!'

Galaxy hiccups, tearing space's seams,
With each odd twist, we're lost in dreams.
Stars wear glasses, a sight so rare,
In this wacky universe, none compare!

Whimsical Worlds Among the Stars

In a land where the comets wear shoes,
And the satellites sing silly blues,
Jupiter jumps with a jaunty flair,
While Saturn spins in polka dot underwear.

Venus giggles, its clouds made of fluff,
Uranus twirls, saying that's quite enough!
Mars has a dance-off with old dusty rocks,
As laughter echoes from cheerful moon blocks.

Each planet has quirks, like socks in a wash,
Pluto claims fame with a shy little posh,
Together they leap on a galactic slide,
In this jolly realm, all concerns they hide.

Stars chuckle softly, their twinkles in sync,
As meteors fly by with a wink and a blink,
In this merry chaos of cosmic delight,
Who knew the universe could be so light!

Celestial Mismatches

A sunbeam wears oversized shades at noon,
While a black hole hums a jazzy tune,
They dance on the rings of a faraway star,
Sipping stardust smoothies, oh how bizarre!

Mercury's got socks that don't match, my friend,
While Venus makes pizzas with a twist at the end,
Earth throws a party, all plants got their sprout,
While Neptune just wonders what life's all about.

Mars wears a cape, claims he flies through the air,
While Jupiter laughs, setting up a fair,
Uranus brings games that are wildly absurd,
The fun never stops, it's the silliest word!

In a whimsy of planets, mismatched and bright,
Each day is a circus, a joyous delight,
They twirl, they bounce, they party each night,
In mismatched universe, everything feels right!

Raucous Radiance of Nebulae

Nebula clouds with colors so loud,
Laughing together, forming quite a crowd,
With stars that burst in a glittery glow,
They throw a big bash, and say, "Let's go!"

One supernova brings cake made of light,
While shooting stars play tag throughout the night,
Each twinkle gets caught in our astral charade,
As we dance like it's all just a grand parade.

Galaxies giggle, their spirals in whirl,
With black holes who munch on a cosmic pearl,
Planets high-fiving in joy up above,
In this raucous wonder of stellar love.

So raise up your voices to skies filled with cheer,
For in the nebulae, nonsense draws near,
With radiant laughter ringing from afar,
Who knew the universe was such a bizarre?

The Misfits of the Milky Way

Among the stars, the misfits convene,
With space boots too large, they frolic unseen,
There's a comet that trips over its tail,
While a starfish on Mars cracks a joke without fail.

Pluto claims wisdom, though small and quite shy,
Riding on meteors, oh my oh my!
With a wink from Orion, they start up a jam,
To the rhythm of lightyears, they go, "Look at them!"

Asteroids dance in a clumsy parade,
While Saturn gets tangled, no need to be afraid,
They all share a laugh at the oddness of fate,
In their galactic circus, it's never too late.

So join in the fun of this cosmic ballet,
With misfits who shine in a peculiar way,
In the heart of the Milky, they find their own beat,
In this stellar wonder, they dance on their feet!

Ecliptic Adventures in Weirdness

Around the sun, they dance with glee,
Planets in a wobbly spree.
Jupiter wearing a funny hat,
Saturn giggling, imagine that!

Comets swing like kids at play,
While asteroids can't find their way.
Venus trips and trips again,
Leaving beauty marks on Mars's den!

Nebulas blend colors bright,
Stardust sprinkles, such a sight.
A rogue moon takes a lazy leap,
Chasing meteors in a sleepy sweep.

Join this dance of the cosmic clowns,
Where laughter swirls 'round cheerful towns.
With every twirl and a silly face,
In a universe of fun and grace!

Stars That Thought Differently

Stars gather for a quirky chat,
Bright ideas wear silly hats.
One says, 'Why not shine in green?'
Another giggles, 'I'm quite unseen!'

The sun suggests a shiny play,
'Let's switch roles for a day!'
Mercury blushes, feeling shy,
While Pluto grins, 'I'm still a guy!'

A black hole jokes, 'I'm a vacuum king,'
Swallowing everything with a swing.
Though they all have their own spark,
Together they light up the dark!

In this galaxy of jests and cheer,
Weirdness reigns through every sphere.
So let your thoughts take flight and soar,
In the night where laughter is never poor!

Contrarian Constellations

In a sky filled with ancient tales,
Some stars decide to buck the scales.
Orion wears mismatched shoes,
While Ursa plays some funky blues!

The Big Dipper spills its drink,
Rickety stars that make you think.
Cassiopeia spins in a twist,
Claiming to be an artist's mist!

Perseus argues with his sword,
Saying, 'I'm really quite adored.'
Yet Draco laughs, twisting in loops,
Imitating the Earth's wise troops.

Each constellation breaks the mold,
Telling stories, bright and bold.
So look up high and don't be shy,
Join the stars in their funny sky!

Bumps in the Sky's Blanket

Under a quilt of sparkling dreams,
Bumps appear, bursting at the seams.
A meteorite sings a silly song,
As stardust dances all night long!

A wobbly planet trips on a star,
Saying, 'Catch me if you can, from afar!'
Galaxies giggle, spinning around,
While black holes munch on space-time sound.

Comets wearing polka dots,
Swish by like they're in a plot!
Supernovae throw a glitter ball,
The cosmos joins in, most of all!

Up with the bumps, enjoy the ride,
Through this quirky cosmic tide.
With laughter woven into the night,
Let your spirit take its flight!

Shimmering Surprises within Space

In the starry sky, a cat flies by,
Wearing sunglasses, oh my oh my!
Planets dance with a silly grin,
While comets juggle, they spin and spin.

Asteroids roll like meatballs in soup,
Dancing with aliens in a curious loop.
Spaceships whistle an off-key tune,
Chasing moons and bouncing in June.

The black holes giggle as they pull away,
Sucking in socks that decided to stray.
Cosmic popcorn pops in the night,
A tasty treat in the ether's flight.

So grab your telescope, make it quick,
Join the fun in this cosmic trick.
With stars that wink and planets that slide,
In this universe, laughter will guide.

Push and Pull of the Extraordinary

A rainbow rocket zooms and glows,
It toots its horn as it wildly goes.
Stars tug on comets, they giggle and sway,
In a game of tag they zoom away.

Jellybean moons bounce off the walls,
Shooting stars trip and stumble in falls.
Gravity whispers a silly joke,
As green Martians dance and smoke.

Chasing shadows of quirky light,
A space walrus takes off in flight.
He plays hide-and-seek with a twinkling star,
In the wide expanse where wonders are.

Life's a party on this cosmic ride,
With surprises galore, come for the tide!
Push and pull in a swirl of fun,
In the theater of stars, you're never done.

Lopsided Views from a Celestial Ship

On a tilted ship with a crescent sail,
We drift through wonders, let's set the trail!
Squid and octopus run the crew,
Steering us toward the cosmic zoo.

A starfish plays cards with a space raccoon,
Counting their chips 'neath a cartoon moon.
The captain sings off-key, but who care?
Lopsided laughter fills the air!

Black holes throw parties, we're first in line,
Getting caught by a warp in the vine.
With each sideways glance at this fun-filled view,
We see the spectrum of cosmic hue.

Twisting through laughter in this wild galore,
All the oddities we just can't ignore!
Floating on dreams in our funny little craft,
The joy of the skies, our silly galactic raft.

Galaxies of the Curious

In galaxies filled with bizarre sights,
Curious critters take lunar flights.
Squishy space bunnies eat marshmallow grass,
While robots play hopscotch, oh what a class!

Wobbling planets wear mismatched shoes,
Twirling around in their festive hues.
Each twinkle a giggle, each orbit a cheer,
Celebrating nonsense, loud and clear.

A telescope's lens wakes up the stars,
Inviting the moon to dance with guitars.
With every shake of the cosmic dust,
The chorus of laughter is a playful must.

Galaxies swirl in a funky parade,
Where wishes are made and dreams are played.
Join the ridiculous, come take a peek,
In this whimsical world, it's fun that we seek.

www.ingramcontent.com/pod-product-compliance
Lightning Source LLC
Chambersburg PA
CBHW051700160426
43209CB00004B/973